Starting Off Strong

Middle/High School

Starting Off Strong

Middle/High School

Beginning
Shared Inquiry™
in Your Classroom

The Great Books Foundation
A nonprofit educational organization

Shared Inquiry™ is a trademark of the Great Books Foundation. The contents of this publication include proprietary trademarks and copyrighted materials and may be used or quoted only with permission and appropriate credit to the Foundation.

First Printing

9   8   7   6   5   4   3   2   1

Printed in the United States of America

Published and distributed by

THE GREAT BOOKS FOUNDATION
A nonprofit educational organization

35 East Wacker Drive, Suite 400

Chicago, IL 60601

www.greatbooks.org

CONTENTS

It's not the house we thought we'd get.

THE HOUSE ON MANGO STREET

Sandra Cisneros

We didn't always live on Mango Street. Before that we lived on Loomis on the third floor, and before that we lived on Keeler. Before Keeler it was Paulina, and before that I can't remember. But what I remember most is moving a lot. Each time it seemed there'd be one more of us. By the time we got to Mango Street, we were six—Mama, Papa, Carlos, Kiki, my sister Nenny, and me.

The house on Mango Street is ours, and we don't have to pay rent to anybody, or share the yard with the people downstairs, or be careful not to make too much noise, and there isn't a landlord banging on the ceiling with a broom. But even so, it's not the house we'd thought we'd get.

We had to leave the flat on Loomis quick. The water pipes broke and the landlord wouldn't fix them because the house was too old. We had to leave fast. We were using the washroom next door and carrying water over in empty milk gallons. That's why Mama and Papa looked for a house, and that's why we moved into the house on Mango Street, far away, on the other side of town.

They always told us that one day we would move into a house, a real house that would be ours for always so we wouldn't have to move each year. And our house would have running water and pipes that worked. And inside it would have real stairs, not hallway stairs, but stairs inside like the houses on TV. And we'd have a basement and at least three washrooms so when we took a bath we wouldn't have to tell everybody. Our house would be white with trees around it, a great big yard, and grass growing without a fence. This was the house Papa talked about when he held a lottery ticket, and this was the house Mama dreamed up in the stories she told us before we went to bed.

But the house on Mango Street is not the way they told it at all. It's small and red with tight steps in front and windows so small you'd think they were holding their breath. Bricks are crumbling in places, and the front door is so swollen you have to push hard to get in. There is no front yard, only four little elms the city planted by the curb. Out back is a small garage for the car we don't own yet and a small yard that looks smaller between the two buildings on either side. There are stairs in our house, but they're ordinary hallway stairs, and the house has only one washroom. Everybody has to share a bedroom—Mama and Papa, Carlos and Kiki, me and Nenny.

Once when we were living on Loomis, a nun from my school passed by and saw me playing out front. The laundromat downstairs had been boarded up because it had been robbed two days before, and the owner had painted on the wood YES WE'RE OPEN so as not to lose business.

Where do you live? she asked.

There, I said, pointing up to the third floor.

You live *there*?

There. I had to look to where she pointed—the third floor, the paint peeling, wooden bars Papa had nailed on the windows so we wouldn't fall out. You live *there*? The way she said it made me feel like nothing. *There.* I lived *there*. I nodded.

I knew then I had to have a house. A real house. One I could point to. But this isn't it. The house on Mango Street isn't it. For the time being, Mama says. Temporary, says Papa. But I know how those things go.

"YOU DON'T GET ANYWHERE CHASING STARS."

THE MOTH AND THE STAR

James Thurber

A young and impressionable moth once set his heart on a certain star. He told his mother about this, and she counseled him to set his heart on a bridge lamp instead. "Stars aren't the thing to hang around," she said; "lamps are the thing to hang around." "You get somewhere that way," said the moth's father. "You don't get anywhere chasing stars."

But the moth would not heed the words of either parent. Every evening at dusk, when the star came out, he would start flying toward it, and every morning at dawn he would crawl back home worn out with his vain endeavor.

One day his father said to him, "You haven't burned a wing in months, boy, and it looks to me as if you were never going to. All your brothers have been badly burned flying around street lamps, and all your sisters have been terribly singed flying around house lamps. Come on, now, get out of here and get yourself scorched! A big strapping moth like you without a mark on him!"

The moth left his father's house, but he would not fly around street lamps, and he would not fly around house lamps. He went right on trying to reach the star, which was four and one-third light years, or twenty-five trillion miles, away. The moth thought it was just caught in the top branches of an elm. He never did reach the star, but he went right on trying, night after night, and when he was a very, very old moth he began to think that he really had reached the star, and he went around saying so. This gave him a deep and lasting pleasure, and he lived to a great old age. His parents and his brothers and his sisters had all been burned to death when they were quite young.

Moral: Who flies afar from the sphere of our sorrow is here today and here tomorrow.

MY REASON BEGAN TO MASTER MY DESPONDENCY.

STATE OF AFFAIRS

Daniel Defoe

I now began to consider seriously my condition, and the circumstances I was reduced to; and I drew up the state of my affairs in writing, not so much to leave them to any that were to come after me (for I was like to have but few heirs), as to deliver my thoughts from daily poring upon them and afflicting my mind. And as my reason began now to master my despondency, I began to comfort myself as well as I could, and to set the good against the evil, that I might have something to distinguish my case from worse; and I stated very impartially, like debtor and creditor, the comforts I enjoyed against the miseries I suffered, thus:

Evil	Good
I am cast upon a horrible, desolate island, void of all hope of recovery.	But I am alive and not drowned, as all my ship's company were.

I am singled out and separated, as it were, from all the world, to be miserable.

But I am singled out, too, from all the ship's crew, to be spared from death; and he that miraculously saved me from death, can deliver me from this condition.

I am divided from mankind, a solitaire; one banished from human society.

But I am not starved and perishing in a barren place, affording no sustenance.

I have no clothes to cover me.

But I am in a hot climate, where, if I had clothes, I could hardly wear them.

I am without any defence or means to resist any violence of man or beast.

But I am cast on an island where I see no wild beasts to hurt me, as I saw on the coast of Africa, and what if I had been shipwrecked there?

I have no soul to speak to or relieve me.

But God wonderfully sent the ship in near enough to the shore, that I have got out so many necessary things, as will either supply my wants or enable me to supply myself, even as long as I live.

THE BOAR WAS THERE SOMEWHERE.

Boar Out There

Cynthia Rylant

Everyone in Glen Morgan knew there was a wild boar in the woods by the Miller farm. The boar was out beyond the splintery rail fence and past the old black Dodge that somehow had ended up in the woods and was missing most of its parts.

Jenny would hook her chin over the top rail of the fence, twirl a long green blade of grass in her teeth and whisper, "Boar out there."

And there were times she was sure she heard him. She imagined him running heavily through the trees, ignoring the sharp thorns and briars that raked his back and sprang away trembling.

She thought he might have a golden horn on his terrible head. The boar would run deep into the woods, then rise up on his rear hooves, throw his head toward the stars and cry a long, clear, sure note into the air. The note would glide through the night and spear the heart of the moon. The boar had no fear of the moon, Jenny knew, as she lay in bed, listening.

One hot summer day she went to find the boar. No one in Glen Morgan had ever gone past the old black Dodge and beyond, as far as she knew. But the boar was there somewhere, between those awful trees, and his dark green eyes waited for someone.

Jenny felt it was she.

Moving slowly over damp brown leaves, Jenny could sense her ears tingle and fan out as she listened for thick breathing from the trees. She stopped to pick a teaberry leaf to chew, stood a minute, then went on.

Deep in the woods she kept her eyes to the sky. She needed to be reminded that there was a world above and apart from the trees—a world of space and air, air that didn't linger all about her, didn't press deep into her skin, as forest air did.

Finally, leaning against a tree to rest, she heard him for the first time. She forgot to breathe, standing there listening to the stamping of hooves, and she choked and coughed.

Coughed!

And now the pounding was horrible, too loud and confusing for Jenny. Horrible. She stood stiff with wet eyes and knew she could always pray, but for some reason didn't.

He came through the trees so fast that she had no time to scream or run. And he was there before her.

His large gray-black body shivered as he waited just beyond the shadow of the tree she held for support. His nostrils glistened, and his eyes; but astonishingly, he was silent. He shivered and glistened and was absolutely silent.

Jenny matched his silence, and her body was rigid, but not her eyes. They traveled along his scarred, bristling back to his thick hind legs. Tears spilling and flooding her face, Jenny stared at the boar's ragged ears, caked with blood. Her tears dropped to the leaves, and the only sound between them was his slow breathing.

Then the boar snorted and jerked. But Jenny did not move.

High in the trees a bluejay yelled, and, suddenly, it was over. Jenny stood like a rock as the boar wildly flung his head and in terror bolted past her.

Past her . . . .

And now, since that summer, Jenny still hooks her chin over the old rail fence, and she still whispers, "Boar out there." But when she leans on the fence, looking into the trees, her eyes are full and she leaves wet patches on the splintery wood. She is sorry for the torn ears of the boar and sorry that he has no golden horn.

But mostly she is sorry that he lives in fear of bluejays and little girls, when everyone in Glen Morgan lives in fear of him.

THE FIVE GUIDELINES
FOR
SHARED INQUIRY DISCUSSION

1. Read the story twice before participating in the discussion.

2. Discuss only the story everyone has read.

3. Support your ideas with evidence from the story.

4. Listen to other participants and respond to them directly.

5. Expect the leader to only ask questions.

BUILDING YOUR ANSWER

Thinking About Ideas in "The House on Mango Street"

BEFORE THE DISCUSSION

The focus question: *Why isn't the narrator satisfied with the house on Mango Street?*

Your first idea: _____

_____

_____

AFTER THE DISCUSSION

Think about all of the ideas the group has suggested and which one makes the most sense.

Your favorite answer: _____

_____

_____

This makes sense because: _____

_____

_____

BUILDING YOUR ANSWER

Supporting Your Ideas in "The Moth and the Star"

BEFORE THE DISCUSSION

The focus question: *According to the story, would the moth have been better off setting his heart on the star, or on the streetlamp?*

Your first idea: _____

_____

_____

A place in the story that makes you think this: _____

_____

_____

_____ (**page** _____)

AFTER THE DISCUSSION

Now think about all the evidence you have heard and think again about how you would answer the question. The story shows that the moth would have been better off setting his heart on the **STAR / STREETLAMP** (circle one).

The two pieces of evidence that most make you think this:

Evidence 1: _____

_____

_____

_____

Evidence 2: _____

_____

_____

_____

BUILDING YOUR ANSWER

Listening to Others in "State of Affairs"

BEFORE THE DISCUSSION

The focus question: *Does Crusoe think the "goods" of his situation make up for the "evils"?*

Your first idea: _____

_____

_____

A place in the story that makes you think this: _____

_____

_____

_____ **(page _____)**

AFTER THE DISCUSSION

Think about all of the ideas you have heard during the discussion.
Two ideas you heard that make you think more about your answer:

1. _____

_____

_____

_____

2. _____

_____

_____

_____

The answer that makes the most sense to you now:_____

_____

_____

_____

Circle one:

I changed my mind.   **I added more evidence
                                to my first idea.**

BUILDING YOUR ANSWER
Putting It All Together in "Boar Out There"

BEFORE THE DISCUSSION

The focus question: _____

_____

_____

Your first idea: _____

_____

_____

A place in the story that makes you think this: _____

_____

_____

_____ **(page _____)**

AFTER THE DISCUSSION

The answer that makes the most sense to you now:_____

_____

_____

_____

Circle one:

I changed my mind.   **I added more evidence to my first idea.**

Our Collaboration

Think about the past four Shared Inquiry discussions we have had. For each pair of statements, circle the number that best describes the work of our whole group in Shared Inquiry discussion. A ⑤ means you agree strongly with the statement to the left of the row of numbers. A ① means you agree strongly with the statement to the right. We will discuss our responses together so that you can offer examples and suggestions for ways we can all improve.

Almost all of us contribute.	5 4 3 2 1	A few people do most of the talking.
We come up with many different ideas about the story.	5 4 3 2 1	We all tend to say the same thing.
We try to back up our ideas with details from the story.	5 4 3 2 1	We just state our ideas and don't explain where they come from.
We listen and comment on one another's ideas.	5 4 3 2 1	We don't pay much attention to what others say.

When asked, we try to explain our ideas and make them clearer to others.	**5 4 3 2 1**	It's hard for us to say more about our ideas.
We're interested and learn a lot.	**5 4 3 2 1**	We get bored and stop paying attention.

Our goals for next time: _____

_____

_____

_____

GLOSSARY

In this glossary, you'll find definitions for words that you may not know, but that are in the stories you've read. You'll find the meaning of each word as it is used in the story. The word may have other meanings as well, which you can find in a dictionary if you're interested. If you don't find a word here that you're wondering about, go to your dictionary for help.

afflicting: Something that is **afflicting** you is causing great trouble or pain. Drough has been **afflicting** Midewestern farmers this year.

banished: If you are **banished**, you are driven away from a place and ordered not to return. The cat was **banished** from the kitchen after jumping on the counter and eating the turkey. If you repeatedly cause trouble while playing soccer, you might be **banished** by the team.

circumstance: A **circumstance** is a condition connected to an event or a place that makes things turn out a certain way. If you had a party and no one came, one **circumstance** could be that you forgot to send invitations; but if no one came because there was a thunderstorm, then the weather was a **circumstance** out of your control.

creditor: A **creditor** is a person or company to whom money is owed. If you borrow money, you will have to repay your **creditor**. A **creditor** usually charges interest (extra charges for borrowing money) in order to make a profit.

debtor: A **debtor** is a person who owes something to another. A **debtor** must pay back loans, plus interest. If you loan money to a friend, your friend will become your **debtor**.

desolate: A **desolate** place does not have any people in it and seems lonely. If your family moves, your new home may seem **desolate** before the furniture arrives. A street seems **desolate** on a rainy day when no one is outside.

despondency: A person suffering from **despondency** is miserable, depressed, and without hope. If you feel very sad, you might go through a phase of **despondency**, where you don't feel like talking to anyone or playing. After breaking her leg in an accident, my aunt sunk into **despondency**.

impartially: If something is done **impartially**, it is done without favoring one side or the other. It is a judge's responsibility to make decisions **impartially**. When a parent helps two children solve an argument, he or she must listen to both sides **impartially** before stating an opinion.

impressionable: If you're an **impressionable** person, you're easily influenced by other people or things. The **impressionable** young boy wanted every toy he saw in the department store. The **impressionable** girl fell in love with Shakespeare's sonnets after hearing them read aloud.

singed: If you **singed** something, you burned it slightly. If you stand too close to a flame, you will **singe** your skin. When my father took the pie out of the oven, he was careless and **singed** his arm.

solitaire: In earlier times, a **solitaire** was a person who feels solitary, or alone.

strapping: A person with a **strapping** build is sturdy and strong. The farmer's son was a **strapping** boy with lots of muscles. The elderly man who lived alone sought a **strapping** neighbor to help him mow the lawn and carry his groceries.

sustenance: Something that supports life, like food or air. People who have had operations usually receive **sustenance** from a feeding or breathing tube before they return to good health. The experienced wilderness student was able to find enough **sustenance** in the woods to last the whole camping trip.

Acknowledgments

All possible care has been taken to trace ownership and secure permission for each selection in this series. The Great Books Foundation wishes to thank the following authors, publishers, and representatives for permission to reprint copyrighted material:

THE HOUSE ON MANGO STREET, by Sandra Cisneros. Copyright 1984 by Sandra Cisneros. Reprinted by permission of Susan Bergholtz Agency.

THE MOTH AND THE STAR, by James Thurber. Copyright 1940, 1968 Rosemary A. Thurber. Reprinted by permission of Rosemary A. Thurber and the Barbara Hogenson Agency, Inc.

Boar Out There, from EVERY LIVING THING, by Cynthia Rylant. Copyright 1985 by Cynthia Rylant. Reprinted by permission of Atheneum Books for Young Readers, an imprint of Simon & Schuster Children's Publishing Division.

Illustration Credits

Chris Mould prepared the illustrations. Copyright 2006 by Chris Mould.

Cover art by Stan Fellows. Copyright 2006 by Stan Fellows.